Writing Workbook for Kids with Dyslexia

100 activities to improve writing and reading skills of dyslexic children

VOLUME 2

BrainChild

TABLE OF CONTENTS

Page No.

INTRODUCTION

Dyslexia is a learning disorder. It can be said that a person is dyslexic when they have difficulties reading and understanding what is written.

When a child has dyslexia, it is much more difficult to decode the letters and read fluently. That is why these children often have difficulties following the class.

Dyslexia can be worked to improve the child's reading, writing, and reading comprehension. The best way to work on these exercises with your child is to create a routine and work on one or two exercises each day.

Exercises to practice writing are covered in this volume and then a complementary activity to practice with the letters learned.

Never put excessive pressure on the child. Patience should be our word mantra. Keep in mind that for the child an exercise that you consider easy is very hard for them.

Focus on the child's small advances. Power your effort and less your results. Do everything you can so that they don't feel bad. Keep in mind that the child is making a great effort.

When we suspect that our child may be dyslexic, we can do a series of activities that will improve their literacy level. Whether in the end, the diagnosis is confirmed or discarded, it will still be very beneficial to facilitate their learning experience.

The important thing is to carry out this type of training before the age of 8 or 9, preferably during the last year of pre-school and the first year of primary school, without taking into account that from school there is still no warning.

In any case, we cannot wait for the diagnosis to be confirmed because we will have missed the best time to intervene and prepare the child to learn to read, and we will have a serious problem if they start 3rd grade and we have not yet intervened the dyslexia, since the increase in school demands will make the problem visible.

In this book and the other volumes of BrainChild, you will find a multitude of resources to work with dyslexia both at school and at home. The exercises have been carried out under the supervision of psychologists and educators.

VOWELS

Vowels of the Alphabet

Short Vowel Sounds

cat

net

igloo

log

sun

a e i o u

Vowels

Long Vowel Sounds

cake

leaf

fire

home

glue

Short Vowel Words			
ant	bad	van	grab
bed	jet	egg	bell
hill	pin	sip	dish
mop	dot	fox	stop
rub	nut	cub	hunt

Long Vowel Words			
make	case	vase	take
eat	pea	meal	beat
bike	dive	like	wipe
too	dose	coat	dome
duty	cube	june	flute

Look at the pictures. Complete the words with the correct short vowels.

b __ g	c __ b	b __ g
b __ t	k __ d	cl __ ck
b __ s	j __ m	m __ p

Activity 2 Long Vowels Review

Look at the pictures. Complete the words with the correct short vowels.

r __ se	t __ ad	r __ ke
wh __ le	l __ ght	t __ a
b __ e	k __ te	fl __ te

Activity 3　Matching Vowel Sounds

Read the words on the right. Match them to the correct vowel sounds.

short a   ●

long a   ●

short e   ●

long e   ●

short i   ●

long i   ●

short o   ●

long o   ●

short u   ●

long u   ●

● bell

● coat

● mitt

● fox

● bean

● man

● cute

● cub

● night

● vase

Activity 4

Magic "e"

Read the short vowel words. Add the magic vowel "e" to make a long vowel word.

Short Vowel Word	Add Magic "e"	Short Vowel Word	Add Magic "e"
at	at ___	hat	hat ___
mat	mat ___	fat	fat ___
mad	mad ___	pin	pin ___
tap	tap ___	sit	sit ___
bit	bit ___	quit	quit ___
rid	rid ___	slim	slim ___
kit	kit ___	cop	cop ___
on	on ___	mop	mop ___
not	not ___	slop	slop ___
hop	hop ___	hug	hug ___
us	us ___	cut	cut ___
tub	tub ___	cub	cub ___

Read and Write

Read the words listed below. Write each short vowel word in the flower and each long vowel word on the leaf.

mop	cage	pen	side
meat	cut	bite	tap
hat	hope	cube	pin

Circle the Vowels

Find and circle all the vowels that you see.

```
    z       i   e       s
e       o   c       u       d

l       z   d   e       a

i   r       o       u       q

o       p   y       s       t

e   s       y       t       i

z       i       o       u       b

g   k       q       e       a

    f       o       d   u   n
```

CONSONANTS

Consonants of the Alphabet

Bb   Cc   Dd   Ff   Gg   Hh

Jj   Kk   Ll   Mm   Nn   Pp

Qq   Rr   Ss   Tt   Vv   Ww

Xx   Yy   Zz

Comman Consonant Blends

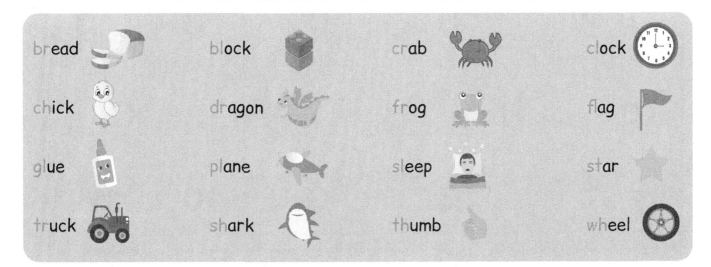

bread	block	crab	clock
chick	dragon	frog	flag
glue	plane	sleep	star
truck	shark	thumb	wheel

Activity 1   Circle the Consonants

Circle the consonants that you see.

h   i   b   c   o

u   y   c   n   a

u   z   x   e   t

q   k   p   s   p

a   r   v   j   u

w   i   p   a   q

o   h   j   l   x

f   e   d   o   w

Activity 2 Beginning Consonants

Look at the pictures. Complete the words with the correct beginning consonants.

__ ebra

__ lass

__ ion

__ able

__ uitar

__ ettle

__ uck

__ all

__ arrot

Activity 3 Ending Consonants

Say the name of the pictures out loud. Circle the letter that makes the ending sounds for each picture.

h d g	m n k	o d l
r b s	r w l	m c n
f t r	x v z	n j m

Draw a line to match the letter to the picture that begins with that initial consonant sound.

H   •

T   •

C   •

P   •

B   •

L   •

N   •

S   •

Activity 5   Beginning Blends

Look at the pictures. Fill in the blanks with the letters that make the beginning blends of consonants.

_____ ock

_____ ant

_____ ider

_____ ark

_____ obe

_____ ule

_____ iken

_____ ar

_____ air

_____ ower

_____ apes

_____ issor

_____ istle

_____ ky

_____ eep

_____ ee

3 SYLLABIC AWARENESS

A word that contains a vowel or, in spoken language, a vowel sound.

One Syllable Words	Two Syllable Words	Three Syllable Words
cat	win-dow	ca-len-der
red	doc-tor	hap-pi-ness
hit	ro-bot	ho-li-day
ten	win-ter	mu-si-cal
see	gar-den	la-dy-bug
toy	pa-per	di-no-saur
zoo	pur-ple	pan-ca-ke
car	wa-ter	but-ter-fly
bad	rab-bit	po-ta-to
sip	but-ton	com-pu-ter
run	pic-nic	um-bre-lla

Activity 1 — One Syllable Words

Find and color the one syllable words.

bed	attack	fish	page	rabbit
cooler	fat	rain	zebra	grow
gan	vase	sick	spider	father
please	thank	water	kick	mood
pat	game	pig	hint	pencil
pen	pea	color	ask	chair

Activity 2   Missing Letters

Look at the picture. Complete the one syllable words with the appropriate letters.

v ___ n

b ___ ll

___ nt

f ___ x

ic ___

f ___ sh

p ___ g

k ___ ng

s ___ x

j ___ mp

m ___ g

b ___ g

Activity 3   Two Syllable Words

Read the words. Find two syllable words from the given words. Write them down.

bag   tiger   ketchup   pet   sister

jacket   ask   net   cat

plan   cartoon   paper   toy   castle

happy   bug   sick   pencil

number   door   candy   honey   cane

table   season   pilot   one

_____   _____   _____

_____   _____   _____

_____   _____   _____

_____   _____   _____

Activity 4 — Write Two Syllables

Read each word and write the syllables on the given lines. One is done for you.

little   lit   tle

puppy   _____   _____

pizza   _____   _____

kitten   _____   _____

honey   _____   _____

yellow   _____   _____

apple   _____   _____

carrot   _____   _____

Activity 5　Two-Syllables Division

Find and circle the word that is divided into correct syllables. Write its letters in the given boxes.

a. na-pkin　　b. nap-kin　　napkin

a. ten-nis　　b. te-nnis

a. go-blin　　b. gob-lin

a. pa-rty　　b. par-ty

a. ro-cket　　b. roc-ket

a. par-rot　　b. pa-rrot

a. pi-rate　　b. pira-te

a. pea-nut　　b. peanu-t

a. app-le　　b. ap-ple

a. ba-by　　b. bab-y

Activity 6 — Match and Color

Match the correct syllables to make a syllable word. Color each syllable of the word the same color and write it in the box. Use a different color for each word that you make.

pi	ket		pirate
pump	dle		
mar	to		
star	kin		
can	boat		
wa	rate		
in	fish		
fun	ter		
sail	ny		

Read each word. Identify the number of syllables in the given word. Write the number of syllables in the box. Also write its syllables on the line.

hotel	2	ho - tel	bee	
body			button	
funny			robot	
coffee			ant	
box			coat	
enjoy			sleepy	
picnic			man	
forest			study	
cane			travel	

Activity 8   Write Syllables

Read each two syllable words below. Say each word then write into syllables.

a.	rocket	roc	–	ket
b.	dinner		–	
c.	panther		–	
d.	turtle		–	
e.	eagle		–	
f.	bubble		–	
g.	candy		–	
h.	hello		–	
i.	monkey		–	
j.	ladder		–	
k.	older		–	
l.	cherry		–	

Activity 9 — Matching Syllables

Draw a line to match the two syllables to make a word. Write the complete word in the given box.

can •	• ten	candy
bas •	• dy	
mit •	• der	
zeb •	• per	
mag •	• za	
gar •	• ra	
spi •	• net	
piz •	• den	
bal •	• ket	
pa •	• loon	

Activity 10 3-Syllable Words

Read each word. Circle the ones that contain three syllables.

daffodil	Computer	hope	family
cane	ladybug	acorn	donut
butterfly	strawberry	rainbow	bank
jellyfish	triangle	potato	stood
eleven	afternoon	light	water
december	desk	library	banana
radio	want	test	monday
cupcake	fantastic	golf	bedroom
card	today	elephant	zebra

Activity 11 Write 3 Syllables

Read each word and write the syllables on the given lines. One is done for you.

for - get - ful	for	get	ful
sep - tem - ber			
car - pen - ter			
te - le - phone			
gar - de - ner			
fa - mi - ly			
ho - li - day			
me - di - cine			

Activity 12 Syllable Sorting

Read the words in the box. Count the syllables in each word and sort them into the proper list.

desk   cupcake   treat   family   onion

flame   banana

hotdog

radio   nose

rocket   hill

pencil   midnight

butterfly

cart   stop

umbrella

1-Syllable Words   2-Syllable Words   3-Syllable Words

_____   _____   _____

_____   _____   _____

_____   _____   _____

_____   _____   _____

_____   _____   _____

Activity 13   How Many Syllables?

Read each word. Identify the number of syllables in the word. Write the number of syllables in the box.

 onion

 asteroid

 crayon

 notebook

 octopus

 rainbow

 sandwich

 detective

 bunny

 triangle

 light

 bedroom

 butterfly

 shock

 time

 dog

Activity 14   Divide and Write

Divide each word into syllables by putting a dash (—) between each syllable.

angry	ang - ry	cupcake	
drink		pajama	
awesome		excited	
winter		oranges	
bitter		gravity	
break		calender	
corner		potato	
good		anyway	
milkshake		flower	
parent		undo	
hundred		starfish	

Activity 15   Animal Syllables

Look at the picture. Say the word aloud and circle the number of how many syllables you hear in the word.

panda 1 2 3	elephant 1 2 3	camel 1 2 3
kangaroo 1 2 3	tiger 1 2 3	koala 1 2 3
lamb 1 2 3	monkey 1 2 3	rabbit 1 2 3

Activity 16   Clapping Out Syllables

Say the word aloud and clap your hands for each syllable. Circle the clapping hands corresponding to the number of syllables. Write the syllables for each word on the line.

Words	1	2	3	Syllables
a. mimic	(👏)	(👏)	👏	mi – mic
b. blow	👏	👏	👏	_____
c. bunny	👏	👏	👏	_____
d, halloween	👏	👏	👏	_____
e. alien	👏	👏	👏	_____
f. cookie	👏	👏	👏	_____
g. jump	👏	👏	👏	_____
h. bank	👏	👏	👏	_____
i. strawberry	👏	👏	👏	_____

Activity 17 Find a Way

Help the little kids find a way to their school by coloring in the boxes that contain two syllable words. You can move up, down or across.

happy	fish	calender
kid	gallop	teacher	water
whale	radio	fantastic	yellow
grand	library	silly	zebra
maple	hotdog	magnet	cup
jungle	tomato	pig	net
cable	little	narrow	personal
pat	beautiful	pumpkin	

Fruit Syllables

Say the word aloud and clap the syllables. Color an apple for each syllable.
Circle the number.

a. pineapple	🍎	🍎	🍎	1	2	3
b. strawberry	🍎	🍎	🍎	1	2	3
c. melon	🍎	🍎	🍎	1	2	3
d. cherries	🍎	🍎	🍎	1	2	3
e.	🍎	🍎	🍎	1	2	3
f. orange	🍎	🍎	🍎	1	2	3
g. peach	🍎	🍎	🍎	1	2	3
h. banana	🍎	🍎	🍎	1	2	3

Activity 19 Count and Check Mark

Read each word and count how many syllables each word has. Put a check mark in the correct box.

Words	1-Syllable	2-Syllables	3-Syllables
a. doctor	☐	☐	☐
b. bear	☐	☐	☐
c. twelve	☐	☐	☐
d. lunch	☐	☐	☐
e. truck	☐	☐	☐
f. computer	☐	☐	☐
g. guitar	☐	☐	☐
h. thin	☐	☐	☐
i. weather	☐	☐	☐
j. summer	☐	☐	☐
k. animal	☐	☐	☐
l. paper	☐	☐	☐

Activity 20   Find and Color

Say each word aloud. Color 1-syllable words with red, 2-syllables words with blue and 3-syllables words with green.

cloud	allow	donkey	shower
mice	exact	stars	cupcake
cold	chocolate	heart	mailbox
puppy	balloon	key	worm
ladybug	snail	apple	sunflower
bird	napkin	wagon	fox
tree	lemonade	today	elephant
alien	bunny	cookie	octopus
donut	kit	jacket	web
card	photograph	bedroom	pail

Activity 21   Hidden Syllables

Look at the pictures. Indicate the hidden syllable to make a complete word.

ap - _____	_____ - bot	flow - _____	but - _____ - fly
kit - _____	_____ - bug	do - _____	cup - _____
note - _____	c _____ n	den - _____	_____ - ster
pa _____	di - _____ - saur	straw - ber - _____	cook - _____
rab - _____	_____ - dow	daf - ___ - dil	_____ - cil

Activity 22   Order the Syllables

Order the syllables listed below and make a complete word in the space.
Write the number of syllables in each word.

Disorder	Syllables	Words	#
gon - dra	dra - gon	dragon	2
mi - ly - fa			
rel - umb - la			
er - ex - cise			
ta - po - to			
na - na - ba			
bow -rain			
day - mon			
li - day - ho			
ly - jel -fish			
day - to			
ness- hap - pi			
to - vic -ry			
ra - zeb			
book - note			
man - snow			
ra - lib- ry			

 **ONSETS and RIMES**

 An **onset** is the initial consonant(s) sound of a syllable.

Words	Onsets	Words	Onsets
pan	pan	dog	dog
pet	pet	bat	bat
tin	tin	slug	slug
bed	bed	run	run

Rime is the string of letters that follow the onset which contains the vowel and any final consonants.

Words	Rimes	Words	Rimes
pan	pan	dog	dog
pet	pet	bat	bat
tin	tin	slug	slug
bed	bed	run	run

Match and Make

Look at the pictures. Draw lines to match each onset, rime and picture. Write complete word in the box.

Onsets	Rimes	Pictures	Words
c	an	🐱	cat
f	og	🎩	
l	ed	🐸	
n	ap	🥅	
b	at	🛏️	
fr	ig	🫐	
h	dog	🐭	
f	eg	🧢	
r	et	🦵	
c	at	🪭	

Activity 2 Build "at" Words

Look at the pictures. Fill in the blanks with the correct onset to complete the word.

f	at	////	flat
	at		
	at		
	at		
	at		
	at		
	at		
	at		
	at		
	at		

Activity 3

Write Rimes

Look at the pictures. Fill in the blanks with the correct rimes to complete the word.

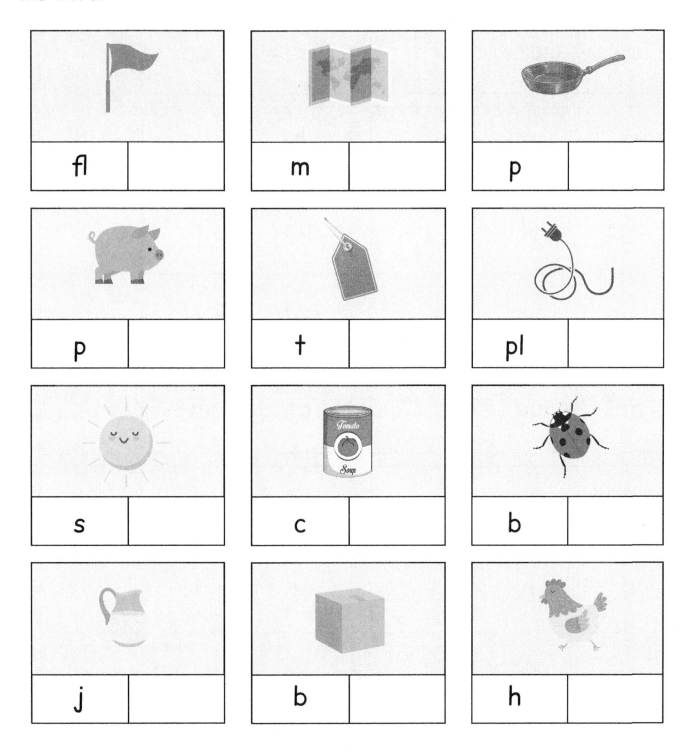

fl		m		p	
p		t		pl	
s		c		b	
j		b		h	

Activity 4

Identify and Color

Color the onset box with green and the rime box with blue. Write the complete word in the blanks.

p	et	

c	ar	

et	n	

b	un	

ug	sl	

un	r	

c	at	

op	t	

m	ug	

at	h	

at	s	

og	l	

ig	p	

an	f	

f	ig	

c	an	

Read the words and write the onset and rime in the columns correctly.

Words	Onsets	Rimes
jam		
icon		
upon		
smug		
twig		
dig		
man		
quit		
den		

PHONEMES

 A phoneme is the most single sound in a word and it allows us to know how to make a word.

EXAMPLE:

The first sound in "hat" is /h/.
The sounds in "hat" are /h/ /a/ /t/ .

The word dog is made up of three Phonemes.
/d/ /o/ /g/

Phonemic Awareness Activities

- Phoneme Isolation

- Phoneme Identification

- Phoneme Categorization

- Phoneme Blending

- Phoneme Segmentation

- Phoneme Deletion

- Phoneme Addition

- Phoneme Substitution

Sounds

Phoneme Isolation

Recognizing individual sounds in a word.

EXAMPLE:

The first sound in pet is /p/.

The middle sound in pet is /e/.

The last sound in pet is /t/.

Words	Beginning Sounds	Middle Sounds	Ending Sounds
cat	/c/	/a/	/t/
bat	/b/	/a/	/t/
sat	/s/	/a/	/t/
sun	/s/	/u/	/t/
bun	/b/	/u/	/n/
bat	/b/	/a/	/t/
map	/m/	/a/	/p/
fog	/f/	/o/	/g/
pin	/p/	/i/	/n/
van	/v/	/a/	/n/

Beginning Sounds

Read the words. What is the first sound in each word? Write it in the given box.

tiger /t/	bed	lamp	log
lion	top	pencil	jam
pig	bell	hut	car
snake	bus	kitten	fan

Activity 2　Ending Sounds

Say the name of each picture aloud. Circle the correct ending sound for each picture.

/g/　/d/　/o/

/h/　/n/　/c/

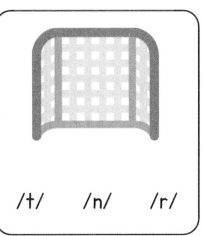

/t/　/n/　/r/

/t/　/r/　/o/

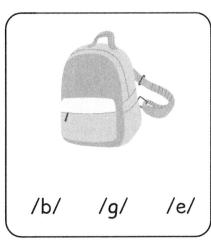

/b/　/g/　/e/

/n/　/d/　/l/

/b/　/d/　/f/

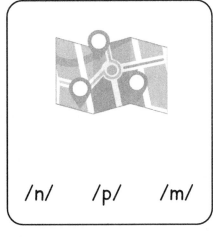

/n/　/p/　/m/

/n/　/a/　/t/

Activity 3   Find and Write

Say the name of each picture. Find and write the /g/ sound in each picture below where you hear it.

Say the name of each picture. Find and write the /s/ sound in each picture below where you hear it.

Activity 4   Find and Circle

Say the name of each picture. Circle each picture that has the /f/ sound somewhere in its name.

Activity 5

Read and Write

Read the words. Write the beginning, middle and ending sound of each word in the correct column.

Words	Beginning Sounds	Middle Sounds	Ending Sounds
bug	/b/	/u/	/g/
tan			
cup			
cat			
mad			
dig			
kite			
top			
sack			
cat			
ten			

Phoneme Identification

Identifying the same sounds in different words

EXAMPLE:

What sound is the same in "pan", "pet", and "pot"?

The first sound /p/ is the same.

Words	Same Sound
map, sap, lap, cap	/a/ , /p/
pet, met, peg, leg	/e/
pot, coat, log, not	/o/
pale, lane, vase, man	/a/
set, bet, met, pet	/e/ , /t/
fan, can, man, pan	/a/ , /n/
sun, sip, snow, spin	/s/
pay, say, way, hay	/a/ , /y/
car, bar, stir, star	/r/
met, pot, not, bet	/t/
sip, dip, dig, lip	/i/

Activity 1   Find and Circle

Read the words. Find and circle the words with the same sound in each row.

cot	can	rot	pot	let	got
say	pay	men	cry	pin	hay
met	pet	beg	let	bag	get
sail	paid	jail	gain	lame	pain
take	safe	late	can	gave	make
few	dew	flew	due	meow	tune
car	arm	park	corn	farm	mole
for	fork	pot	star	corn	sort
can	man	pen	leg	tan	tiny

Activity 2 — Identify and Write

Read the words. Identify the same sound in the different words and write it in the blanks.

Words				Same Sounds
met	cat	sit	bet	
car	bar	star	ear	
got	loan	bone	fog	
peg	beg	leg	neg	
kid	mad	cud	rod	
fell	sell	ball	mall	
bat	cat	hat	mat	
ride	bad	bird	loud	
loss	pom	pot	slob	
boar	four	roar	core	
foam	roam	boat	coat	

Activity 3 Say and Write

Look at the pictures and say the name of each picture aloud. Write the same sound that you hear in each picture.

_____

_____

_____

_____

_____

_____

Phoneme Categorization

Identifying the word in a set of three or more words that has an odd sound.

EXAMPLE:

Which word has an odd sound? pet, mug, pan

'mug' has an odd sound. It does not start with /p/.

Spot the "odd" one out!

tree	feet	(flew)	sleep
mat	pat	cat	pin
frog	play	stay	hay
stop	mop	slope	alive
can	dig	car	cap
sun	smoke	star	moon
seat	meat	grow	neat

Activity 1   Odd One Out

Read the words. Cross out the one that has an odd sound. Write the same sound that does not belong to the odd one.

sheep	sleep	~~car~~	jeep	/ee/ /p/
cat	mat	bell	pat	
jam	ram	pen	calm	
map	snap	cap	rat	
know	grow	show	seat	
mug	man	nest	map	
leg	got	log	lip	
pay	mole	say	hay	
bus	cat	bug	bag	
dig	dog	lap	dam	

Activity 2   Find and Color

Read the words. Find and color the word in each row that has an odd sound.

sip	flip	man	clip	sun	dip
bat	can	car	leg	cap	pat
rat	rake	tea	ran	van	rain
log	for	mug	frog	pot	pen
pet	met	let	man	get	can
bee	saw	knee	see	car	mop
jail	hail	bag	mail	bat	sail

Activity 3   Cross Out the Picture

Say the name of each picture aloud. Cross out the picture that has an odd sound in its name.

Phoneme Blending

Listen to a sequence of separate phonemes and combine the phonemes to make a word.

EXAMPLE:

What is the word /r/ /a/ /t/ ?

This is a rat.

Phonemes	Words	
/c/ /a/ /t/	cat	
/a/ /n/ /t/	ant	
/b/ /a/ /t/	bat	
/c/ /a/ /n/	can	
/f/ /a/ /n/	fan	
/t/ /r/ /ee/	tree	
/b/ /e/ /d/	bed	
/s/ /i/ /t/	sit	
/t/ /o/ /p/	top	
/l/ /e/ /g/	leg	
/m/ /a/ /p/	map	
/l/ /i/ /p/	lip	

Activity 1   Sounds and Write

Look at the picture and say the word. Sound it out and circle the sounds. Write the word.

Say	Sound it Out			Write
	ch i	e ck	oo n	
	c e	b o	l ck	
	b e	oo ck	k c	
	i e	g l	a oo	
	p i	l n	a t	
	r o	o t	b n	

Activity 2   Matching Blends

Draw a line to match the phonemes to the correct words.

/f/ /a/ /s/ /t/   ●   cow

/l/ /o/ /ck/   ●   ● crash

/r/ /a/ /t/   ●   ● dress

/c/ /a/ /r/ /d/   ●   ● chip

/d/ /r/ /e/ /ss/   ●   ● fast

/c/ /ow/   ●   ● lock

/c/ /r/ /a/ /sh/   ●   ● rat

/ch/ /i/ /p/   ●   ● queen

/k/ /i/ /t/   ●   ● card

/d/ /o/ /g/   ●   ● kit

/qu/ /ee/ /n/   ●   ● dog

Activity 3   Make a Word

Look at the pictures. Blend each word by drawing a line to the matching phoneme. Write the word.

	/p/ /e/ /g/ /c/ /i/ /d/			pig
	/a/ /l/ /s/ /s/ /o/ /ck/			
	/c/ /l/ /a/ /s/ /ou/ /d/			
	/f/ /e/ /o/ /c/ /l/ /ck/			
	/h/ /r/ /t/ /n/ /a/ /m/			
	/s/ /d/ /a/ /a/ /n/ /t/			
	/p/ /l/ /s/ /v/ /a/ /t/			
	/d/ /l/ /r/ /s/ /oo/ /ck/			
	/f/ /y/ /c/ /i/ /sh/ /k/			

Phoneme Segmentation

Breaking a word down into its individual sounds and saying each sound as it is tapped out or counted.

EXAMPLE:

How many sounds are in "plant" ?

Five sounds /p/ /l/ /a/ /n/ /t/.

Words	Sounds	Number of Sounds
cat	/k/ /a/ /t/	three
ant	/a/ /n/ /t/	three
bat	/b/ /a/ /t/	three
cow	/k/ /ow/	two
fan	/f/ /a/ /n/	three
tree	/t/ /r/ /ee/	three
park	/p /ar/ /k/	three
sit	/s/ /i/ /t/	three
top	/t/ /o/ /p/	three
bee	/b/ /ee/	two
map	/m/ /a/ /p/	three
lip	/l/ /i/ /p/	three

Activity 1   Say and Write

Say the name of each picture. Separate the words into their individual sounds. Write each sound in its box.

	/a/	/n/	/t/	

Activity 2   Count and Write

Say the name of each picture. Write the number of sounds you hear in the box.

Activity 3   Missing Sounds

Say the name of each picture. Look at the sounds underneath. Fill in the missing sounds.

/n/		/t/	/k/	/u/			/u/	/n/
/n/	/u/			/e/			/a/	/r/
	/i/		/h/			/w/		/b/
	/a/		/m/		/g/	/p/		/n/
/b/				/a/				/g/

Say the name of each picture. Color in each star for each sound that you hear. Write the segments in the given box.

Activity 5   Say and Match

Say the name of each picture. Break the words down into their individual sounds. Match each picture to the correct sounds.

     ●   ●   /k/ /oa/ /t/

     ●   ●   /d/ /r/ /u/ /m/

   ●   ●   /s/ /k/ /a/ /l/

     ●   ●   /s/ /n/ /a/ /il/

     ●   ●   /f/ /l/ /a/ /g/

   ●   ●   /t/ /e/ /n/ /t/

     ●   ●   /h/ /a/ /n/ /d/

                                          ●   /t/ /r/ /u/ /ck/

Activity 6　Matching Sounds

Draw a line to match the words to their correct sounds.

jet	/s/ /u/ /n/
land	/f/ /a/ /t/
noise	/s/ /o/ /k/
pick	/s/ /l/ /e/ /d/
cat	/b/ /i/ /g/
bike	/d/ /o/ /n/
sock	/n/ /oi/ /z/
sun	/p/ /i/ /k/
fat	/s/ /p/ /i/ /n/
sled	/y/ /e/ /l/
big	/k/ /a/ /t/
spin	/l/ /a/ /n/ /d/
yell	/b/ /i/ /k/
ran	/j/ /e/ /t/
dawn	/r/ /a/ /n/

Phoneme Deletion

Identifying the word that remains when a phoneme is removed from another word.

EXAMPLE:

What is "train" without "t"?

Train without "t" is "rain".

Words	Words without "d"
dice	ice
dinner	inner
card	car
seed	see
dart	art
draw	raw
drag	rag

Delete the sound in the box from each of the following words. Write the new word on the line.

bust - /t/ _____

crab - /r/ _____

cane - /e/ _____

heat - /h/ _____

block - /b/ _____

farm - /f/ _____

dear - /d/ _____

mice - /m/ _____

tear - /t/ _____

bust - /t/ _____

clock - /c/ _____

black - /b/ _____

late - /l/ _____

stop - /s/ _____

mart - /m/ _____

clap - /c/ _____

train - /t/ _____

plane - /p/ _____

smile - /s/ _____

trust - /t/ _____

Activity 2   Matching Words

Draw a line to match the following words with the new words.

braid - /b/	ink
trace - /t/	ate
fear - /f/	raid
rice - /r/	row
twig - /t/	race
slip - /s/	ear
grain - /g/	can
crow - /c/	rain
gate - /g/	wug
link - /l/	ice
cane - /e/	lip

Activity 3   Delete and Make

1. Delete the /b/ sound from each of the following words. Make new words and write them on the line.

a. bend _____   b. bare _____

c. band _____   d. blame _____

2. Delete the /t/ sound from each of the following words. Make new words and write them on the line.

a. tall _____   b. train _____

c. seat _____   d. pant _____

3. Delete the /m/ sound from each of the following words. Make new words and write them on the line.

a. storm _____   b. calm _____

c. more _____   d. mate _____

4. Delete the /r/ sound from each of the following words. Make new words and write them on the line.

a. cart _____   b. crab _____

c. grain _____   d. liver _____

5. Delete the /s/ sound from each of the following words. Make new words and write them on the line.

a. snail _____   b. strap _____

c. struck _____   d. stop _____

Phoneme Addition

Making a new word by adding a phoneme to an existing word.

EXAMPLE:

Which word will we get by adding /c/ to "lever"?

The new word is "clever" by adding /c/ to "lever".

Words	New Words
tick + /s/	stick
pace + /l/	place
lick + /c/	click
amp + /r/	ramp
art + /c/	cart
and + /h/	hand
lock + /c/	clock

Activity 1 Add and Write

Add the sound in the box from each of the following words. Write the new word on the line.

car   +   /t/   _____   art   +   /c/   _____

lamp   +   /c/   _____   tend   +   /r/   _____

eat   +   /s/   _____   can   +   /e/   _____

eat   +   /m/   _____   eat   +   /h/   _____

at   +   /s/   _____   it   +   /s/   _____

arm   +   /f/   _____   teat   +   /r/   _____

end   +   /s/   _____   aid   +   /s/   _____

ice   +   /r/   _____   at   +   /c/   _____

ear   +   /f/   _____   and   +   /s/   _____

end   +   /t/   _____   tail   +   /r/   _____

Activity 2   Matching Words

Draw a line to match the following words with the new words.

and + /b/   slip

pot + /s/   plant

log + /b/   band

lip + /s/   stand

ear + /t/   pink

lip + /f/   brand

win + /t/   tear

pant + /l/   twin

band + /r/   blog

ink + /p/   spot

sand + /t/   flip

Phoneme Substitution

Substituting one phoneme for another to make a new word.

EXAMPLE:

The word is "pet". Change /p/ to /m/.

New word is "met".

cat	change /c/ to /r/	rat
kite	change /k/ to /b/	bite
kit	change /k/ to /s/	sit
men	change /m/ to /p/	pen
ball	change /b/ to /t/	tall
calm	change /c/ to /p/	palm
bag	change /b/ to /t/	tag
clap	change /c/ to /s/	slap
book	change /b/ to /t/	took
seat	change /s/ to /m/	meat

Activity 1 Replace and Make

Replace the beginning sound of each word with a new sound to make a new word that matches the picture. Write the new word in the box.

nail	tie	can
map	hot	bar
lake	hike	lift

Activity 2   Replace and Write

Replace the colored letter with the phoneme in the box. Write each new word on the line.

bag	/t/	_____	fail	/m/	_____
line	/f/	_____	cat	/p/	_____
race	/f/	_____	fail	/m/	_____
harm	/f/	_____	mouse	/h/	_____
pod	/t/	_____	fake	/m/	_____
wood	/f/	_____	bitter	/u/	_____
van	/m/	_____	can	/p/	_____
goat	/b/	_____	rail	/n/	_____
pain	/r/	_____	tall	/b/	_____
slug	/p/	_____	rest	/u/	_____
log	/e/	_____	net	/w/	_____
bear	/t/	_____	slip	/c/	_____

Activity 3   Make New Words

Replace the red colored sound of each word with the /a/ sound to make a new word. Write the new word in the box.

spin

pit

lock

run

sick

pin

hit

mop

spit

like

mile

met

slip

clip

lite

beg

set

line

RHYMES

Rhymes are words that sound similar to each other when you say or hear them.

Rhyming Words

cat	hat	bat
hay	say	day
let	pet	met
cap	map	lap
mall	hall	ball
sun	bun	run
sit	kit	pit

Activity 1 Read and Circle

Read the words. Circle the words in each row that rhyme with the first one in the box.

feet	heat	head	meat

| bone | cone | tone | tune |

| mine | pin | line | fine |

| map | met | cap | lap |

| bed | fed | led | let |

| tub | rub | hub | sub |

| pot | rot | hot | pit |

| cow | con | pow | row |

Activity 2   Matching Picture

Draw a line to match the pictures whose names rhyme with each other.

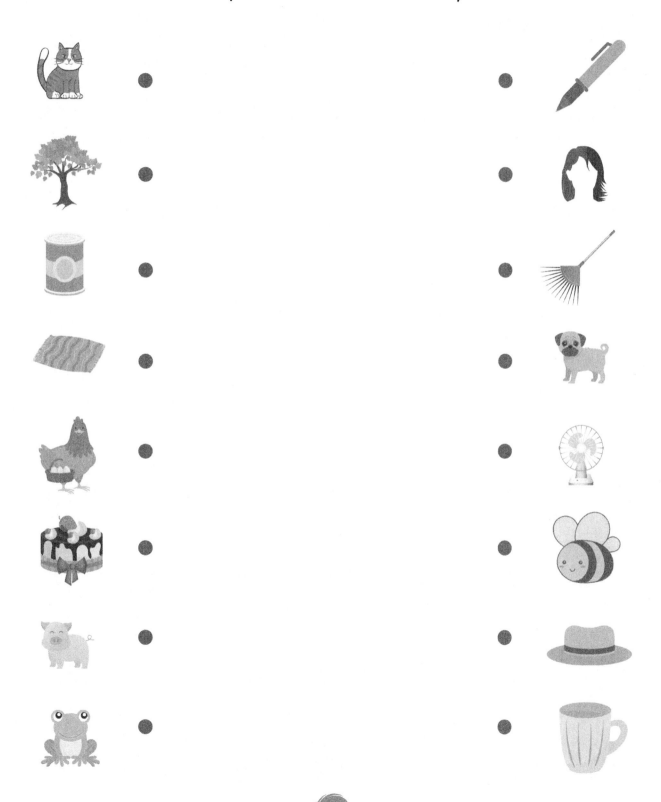

Activity 3

Find and Circle

Find and circle the word in each row that does not rhyme with the others.

tight	eight	light	bright
kite	site	mate	bite
lap	man	cap	map
lock	book	hook	cook
tag	bag	rag	dog
four	door	hour	store
ball	tall	hall	tell
got	let	met	get

Matching Rhymes

Draw a line to match the words that rhyme with each other.

pocket	pump
deep	round
hard	stuck
jump	fame
sound	lane
luck	loud
coat	plug
proud	rocket
lame	sheep
cane	card
slug	float

Activity 5   Missing Letters

Read the word in the box. Fill in the missing letter corresponding to the word it rhymes with in box.

dog

| l __ g | fr __ g | fo __ | __ og |

fed

| __ ed | w __ d | le __ | n __ d |

cat

| p __ t | ma __ | __ at | r __ t |

see

| be __ | k __ ee | t __ ee | ple __ |

sad

| m __ d | __ ad | ha __ | f __ d |

jet

| l __ t | be __ | m __ t | __ et |

kid

| s __ t | __ id | di __ | b __ d |

mug

| j __ g | __ ug | sl __ g | __ lug |

cut

| sh __ t | __ ut | n __ t | gu __ |

Activity 6   Read and Write

Read the word, and write down a word on the line that rhymes with the other.

mope and _____

when and _____

bake and _____

rake and _____

corn and _____

fish and _____

sky and _____

clock and _____

pool and _____

ten and _____

fox and _____

nap and _____

coat and _____

mike and _____

bit and _____

fruit and _____

fan and _____

kite and _____

book and _____

king and _____

cane and _____

jug and _____

Activity 7   Matching Rhymes

Draw a line to match the words that rhyme with each other.

tank   late

jar   lack

gate   bar

back   barn

born   bank

yarn   horn

Activity 8

Make a Rhyme

Look a the pictures and write down three words that rhyme with the given pictures.

Activity 9

Find the Rhyme

Say the name of each picture aloud. Circle the three pictures in each row that rhyme.

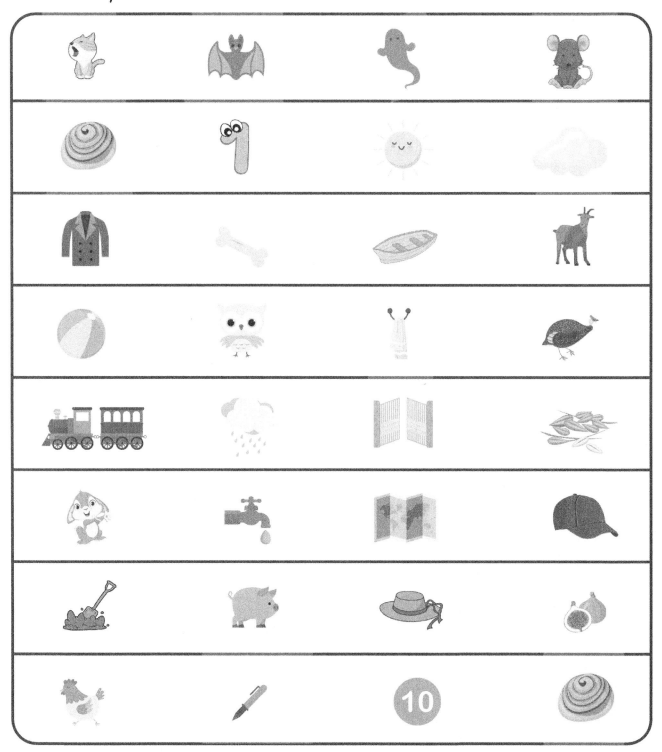

Activity 10   Think and Write

How many rhymes can you think of for each word? Write them down.

lack	
snail	
ice	
plane	
fan	
bit	
knight	
land	
game	
hide	
face	

Look at the pictures. Circle the correct word that rhymes with the picture.

see bat	pin fox	sun bag
fed pet	ram game	bake bike
cut pat	cap sip	fog fig
tie tire	fry bite	fan jam

Activity 12   Find and Sort it

Read the words in the box below. Write the words in the correct column that rhyme with the word found at the top of each column.

zone	take	bore	king

swing   lake   four   phone   bake

cone   lone   fake   sting   loan

make   sing   don   shake   core

roar   sour   wing   pore   ping

ring   tone   for   store   rake

Sight words are commonly used, that appear most frequently when reading any type of writing.

the	that	with
of	in	it
his	he	she
are	is	am
I	to	as
you	have	be
at	was	and

Activity 1   Build Sentences

Write the correct sight words in the boxes to complete the sentences.

have	the	to	are
am	is	see	has

a. I ☐ a cat.

b. I ☐ reading.

c. He ☐ my friend.

d. They ☐ happy.

e. Here is ☐ dog.

f. I like ☐ eat a pizza.

g. I ☐ a bag.

h. She ☐ a pet.

Activity 2   Word Search

Find all the hidden sight words that are listed on the right. Words can go up, down, or across.

p	g	h	s	h	e	f	d
a	f	j	y	d	u	h	u
m	j	h	i	w	s	m	t
g	o	a	t	h	e	s	h
o	b	s	a	n	d	z	a
a	r	e	m	d	m	h	t
q	n	e	f	y	k	r	h
i	s	l	b	f	q	b	x

the

that

is

it

am

are

and

she

has

Complete the sentences with the help of the listed sight words.

I _____ a boy.

Is _____ your bag?

This _____ my house.

Activity 3   Make Sentences

Look at the pictures. Use the sight words to make sentences describing the pictures.

Activity 4   Color by Sight Words

Color the sight words using the color codes listed below.

the	can	and	am	has
am	can	they	the	and
they	and	the	they	has
the	am	they	can	the
they	and	the	has	can

the = green   can = pink   am = blue

and = yellow   has = red   they = orange

Activity 5   Find and Circle

Read the sentences. Circle the sight words in the sentences that you see in the colored box.

a. Lets   go   to   the   park.

b. Look   at   my   new   toy.

c. You   are   my   friend.

d. I   can   see   the   rainbow.

e. Put   the   ball   down.

f. I   like   to   eat   banana.

g. I   have   a   puppy.

h. I   see   a   dog.

i. He   is   my   brother.

j. The   cat   is   black.

k. I   play   the   violin.

my

the

at

I

he

to

is

a

are

you

have

Activity 6   Matching Sight Words

Read the sentences. Draw a line to match the incomplete sentences with the correct sight word to make them complete.

The dog _____ here.   can

_____ is raining.   are

She sits under _____ tree.   they

This is _____ pet.   is

Is _____ your pencil?   it

He is _____ tired.   the

You _____ right.   my

I _____ read a book   very

He is going _____ school.   this

_____ are hapy.   to

Activity 7   Read a Story

Read the story carefully. Write down the sight words that you read in the story.

The Lion and The Mouse

A lion was once sleeping in the jungle when a mouse started running up and down his body just for fun. This disturbed the lion's sleep, and he woke up quite angry. He was about to eat the mouse when the mouse desperately requested the lion to set him free. "I promise you, I will be of great help to you someday if you save me." The lion laughed at the mouse's confidence and let him go.

One day, a few hunters came into the forest and took the lion with them. They tied him up against a tree. The lion was struggling to get out and started to whimper. Soon, the mouse walked past and noticed the lion in trouble. Quickly, he ran and gnawed on the ropes to set the lion free. Both of them sped off into the jungle.

_____ _____ _____ _____

_____ _____ _____ _____

_____ _____ _____ _____

_____ _____ _____ _____

_____ _____ _____ _____

Other BrainChild books available on Amazon

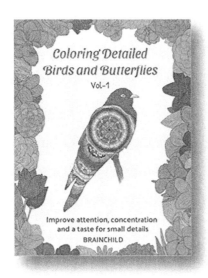

Printed in Great Britain
by Amazon